D0252323

building your
Marriage

By Dennis Rainey

"Unless the Lord builds the house, its builders labor in vain"
(Psalm 127:1a).

FAMILYLIFE™
Bringing Timeless Principles Home
Little Rock, Arkansas

Loveland, Colorado

Group's R.E.A.L. Guarantee to you:

Every Group resource incorporates our R.E.A.L. approach to ministry—a unique philosophy that results in long-term retention and life transformation. It's ministry that's:

**This is EARL.
He's R.E.A.L.
mixed up.
(Get it?)**

Relational
Because student-to-student interaction enhances learning and builds Christian friendships.

Experiential
Because what students experience sticks with them up to 9 times longer than what they simply hear or read.

Applicable
Because the aim of Christian education is to be both hearers and doers of the Word.

Learner-based
Because students learn more and retain it longer when the process is designed according to how they learn best.

Building Your Marriage

Copyright 2000 Dennis Rainey

Visit our Web site: **www.grouppublishing.com**

Credits
FamilyLife
Editor: David Boehi
Assistant Editor: Julie Denker

Group Publishing, Inc.
Editor: Matt Lockhart
Creative Development Editor: Paul Woods
Chief Creative Officer: Joani Schultz
Copy Editor: Bob Kretschman
Art Director: Jenette L. McEntire
Cover Art Director: Jeff A. Storm
Computer Graphic Artist: Anita M. Cook
Cover Photographer: FPG International
Illustrator: Ken Jacobsen
Production Manager: Peggy Naylor

ISBN 0-7644-2237-5
10 9   09 08 07 06 05 04 03

Printed in the United States of America.

How to Let the Lord Build Your House
and not labor in vain

———————————•———————————

The HomeBuilders Couples Series®: A small-group Bible study dedicated to making your family all that God intended.

FamilyLife is a division of Campus Crusade for Christ International, an evangelical Christian organization founded in 1951 by Bill Bright. FamilyLife was started in 1976 to help fulfill the Great Commission by strengthening marriages and families and then equipping them to go to the world with the gospel of Jesus Christ. The FamilyLife Marriage Conference is held in most major cities throughout the United States and is one of the fastest-growing marriage conferences in America today. "FamilyLife Today," a daily radio program hosted by Dennis Rainey, is heard on hundreds of stations across the country. Information on all resources offered by FamilyLife may be obtained by contacting us at the address, telephone number, or World Wide Web site listed below.

Bringing Timeless Principles Home

Dennis Rainey, Executive Director
FamilyLife
P.O. Box 8220
Little Rock, AR 72221-8220
1-800-FL-TODAY
www.familylife.com

A division of Campus Crusade for Christ International
Bill Bright, Founder and President

BUILDING YOUR MARRIAGE

Dedication

To Jerry and Sheryl Wunder
because your friendship, servanthood, and lives have made the
HomeBuilders Couples Series a reality

About the Author

Dennis Rainey is the executive director and co-founder of FamilyLife, a division of Campus Crusade for Christ, and is a graduate of Dallas Theological Seminary. Since 1976, he has overseen the rapid growth of FamilyLife Conferences on marriage and parenting. He is also the daily host of the nationally syndicated radio program "FamilyLife Today." Dennis was the recipient of the National Religious Broadcasters Radio Program Producer of the Year Award for 1995. Dennis serves as a member of the board of directors for the Evangelical Council for Financial Accountability.

Dennis and his wife, Barbara, have spoken at FamilyLife Conferences across the United States and overseas. Dennis is also a speaker for Promise Keepers. He has testified on family issues before Congress and has appeared on numerous radio and television programs.

Dennis and Barbara have co-authored numerous books, including *The New Building Your Mate's Self-Esteem*, *Moments Together for Couples*, *Parenting Today's Adolescent*, and *Two Hearts Are Better Than One*. Dennis has also written *Starting Your Marriage Out Right*, *The Tribute and the Promise* (with David Boehi), *One Home at a Time*, and several studies in the *HomeBuilders Couples Series*.

Dennis and Barbara are both graduates of the University of Arkansas. They have six children and live near Little Rock, Arkansas.

Contents

Acknowledgments 8

Introduction 10

Session One: Overcoming Isolation 13

Session Two: Creating Oneness 25

Session Three: Receiving Your Spouse 35

Session Four: Constructing a Relationship 45

Session Five: Fitting Together...59

Session Six: Building in the Spirit.....................................73

Session Seven: Building a Legacy.......................................85

Where Do You Go From Here? 97

Our Problems, God's Answers 101

Leader's Notes 111

Acknowledgments

The following Bible study is a result of the vision and labor of a team of individuals committed to strengthening marriages around the world. While I owe many thanks to the entire FamilyLife staff, a few "heroes" deserve special recognition.

Since the first version of *Building Your Marriage* was written back in 1987, my friend and colleague Jerry Wunder has been, in many ways, the heart behind this entire project. His unwavering belief in this study endured months of writing, testing, and final reworking. Bob Horner played an instrumental role throughout this process through his vital conceptual and content advice. Robert Lewis, Bill McKenzie, and Lee Burrell also made significant contributions toward the content of the Bible study. Other key people in the development process were Jeff Lord, Mark Dawson, Mike Rutter, Fred Hitchcock, Donna Guirard, Tim Allen, Brenda Harris, and Jeff Tickson.

Don and Sally Meredith have also influenced our ministry and our lives in so many ways and, as a result, leave a legacy through this study.

To Dave Boehi, who had spearheaded our HomeBuilders effort during the last decade, thanks for your commitment to families! You are a HomeBuilder among homebuilders. Thanks, too, for your friendship and truth speaking over the years. You are a good man! It's a privilege to work with you.

Julie Denker has played a critical role in the editing and publishing process of every HomeBuilders study. Through her, hundreds of thousands of lives are being touched every year. Thanks, Julie, for helping make a difference at FamilyLife.

There were many groups around the country that participated

in pilot home studies. Thanks for your feedback. It was invaluable.

Finally, thanks to Dave Thornton, Paul Woods, and Matt Lockhart for your role with Group Publishing as we have revised and updated this study. Your partnership is invaluable.

Introduction

When a man and woman are married, they stand before a room of witnesses and proclaim their commitment to a lifetime of love. They recite a sacred vow "to have and to hold...from this day forward...to love, honor, and cherish...for better, for worse...for richer, for poorer...in sickness and in health...as long as we both shall live."

It's a happy day, perhaps the happiest in their lives. And yet, once the honeymoon ends, once the emotions of courtship and engagement subside, many couples realize that "falling in love" and building a good marriage are two different things. Keeping those vows is much more difficult than they thought it would be.

Otherwise intelligent people who would not think of buying a car, investing money, or even going to the grocery store without some initial planning enter into marriage with no plan of how to make that relationship succeed.

But God has already provided the plan, a set of blueprints for building a truly God-honoring marriage. His plan is designed to enable a man and woman to grow together in a mutually satisfying relationship and then to reach out to others with the love of Christ. Ignoring this plan leads only to isolation and separation between husband and wife. It's a pattern evident in so many homes today: Failure to follow God's blueprints results in wasted effort, bitter disappointment, and, in far too many cases, divorce.

In response to this need in marriages today, FamilyLife has developed a series of small-group studies called the HomeBuilders Couples Series.

You could complete this study alone with your spouse, but we strongly urge you to either form or join a group of couples studying this material. You will find that the questions in each session not only help you grow closer to your spouse, but they help create a special environment of warmth and fellowship as you study together how to build the type of marriage you desire. Participating in a HomeBuilders group could be one of the highlights of your married life.

The Bible: Your Blueprints for a God-Honoring Marriage

You will notice as you proceed through this study that the Bible is used frequently as the final authority on issues of life and marriage. Although written thousands of years ago, this Book still speaks clearly and powerfully about the conflicts and struggles faced by men and women. The Bible is God's Word—his blueprints for building a God-honoring home and for dealing with the practical issues of living.

We encourage you to have a Bible with you for each session. For this series we use the New International Version as our primary reference. Another excellent translation is the New American Standard Bible.

Ground Rules

Each group session is designed to be enjoyable and informative—and nonthreatening. Three simple ground rules will help ensure that everyone feels comfortable and gets the most out of the experience:

1. Don't share anything that would embarrass your spouse.

2. You may pass on any question you don't want to answer.

3. If possible, plan to complete the HomeBuilders Project as a couple between group sessions.

A Few Quick Notes About Leading a HomeBuilders Group

1. Leading a group is much easier than you may think! A group leader in a HomeBuilders session is really a "facilitator." As a leader, your goal is simply to guide the group through the discussion questions. You don't need to teach the material—in fact, we don't want you to! The special dynamic of a HomeBuilders group is that couples teach themselves.

2. This material is designed to be used in a home small group, but it also can be adapted for use in a Sunday school environment. (See page 113 for more information about this option.)

3. We have included a section of Leader's Notes in the back of this book. Be sure to read through these notes before leading a session; they will help you prepare.

4. For more material on leading a HomeBuilders group, be sure to get a copy of the *HomeBuilders Leader's Guide*, by Drew and Kit Coons. This book is an excellent resource that provides helpful guidelines on how to start a study, how to keep discussion moving, and much more.

Overcoming Isolation

Defeating selfishness and isolation is essential in
building oneness and a God-honoring marriage.

W A R M • U P   15   M I N U T E S

Getting to Know You

Introduce yourselves as a couple by telling the group
one of the following things about your relationship
(talk briefly to decide what to share):

- When and where you met.
- One fun or unique date before your marriage.
- One humorous or romantic time from your honey-
  moon or early married life.

Getting Connected

Pass your books around the room, and have each couple
write in their names, phone numbers, and e-mail addresses
in the space provided on the next page.

_____
NAME, PHONE, & E-MAIL

_____
NAME, PHONE, & E-MAIL

_____
NAME, PHONE, & E-MAIL

_____
NAME, PHONE, & E-MAIL

_____
NAME, PHONE, & E-MAIL

_____
NAME, PHONE, & E-MAIL

For Extra Impact

Coin Toss: Use this exercise as a fun way to kick off the study and to help illustrate the issue of selfishness.

Dig out all the coins you can find in your pockets or purse, and put them in a pile between you and your spouse. Then take turns flipping coins—ladies first. If a coin comes up heads, the wife gets to choose a coin to keep; if it's tails, the husband gets to pick. Do this for a couple of minutes, then gather with the other couples, and answer the following questions:

- What emotions did you experience during this exercise?

- What thoughts went through your mind as you decided which coins to keep?

Feelings of selfishness and self-centeredness are natural to all of us but are harmful to the health of a marriage. In this session, we will work on building our marriages by identifying and dealing with selfishness and its effects.

Causes of Failure in Marriage

1. During engagement and early marriage, many couples seem to experience a high level of romance and emotional closeness. But as time goes by, they sometimes feel more distant. Why do you think this happens?

2. One of the main reasons people get married is to find intimacy—a close, personal relationship with another person. Yet most couples find that this type of intimacy does not seem to come naturally. Why do you think this is?

3. Read Isaiah 53:6a. What do you see that helps explain the failure of some marriages to achieve intimacy?

4. What are some ways selfishness is displayed in marriage? What relationship do you see between selfishness and isolation?

Going Your Own Way

5. Selfishness in a relationship leads to isolation, which happens when people in a marriage drift apart from each other. What is the effect of isolation on marriage?

6. Why do you think some people are willing to tolerate isolation instead of working to build oneness and harmony in their marriage?

7. It is often easier to see selfishness in your spouse than in yourself. What are some ways you struggle with being selfish in your marriage? Take a minute to jot down a few things, then share your list with your spouse.

Answer questions 7 and 8 with your spouse. After answering, you may want to share an appropriate insight or discovery with the group.

8. In what ways has "going your own way" affected your marriage?

Hope for Defeating Selfishness and Isolation

9. Read Mark 10:35-45, and see how Jesus dealt with a selfish request. How does this passage apply to your marriage?

10. Read Philippians 2:3-4. What does this passage indicate are some keys to defeating selfishness and overcoming isolation?

Answer the first part of question 11 individually. Then share your answer with your spouse. Work together as a couple to agree on an answer for the second part.

11. What did you learn during this session that can help you build your marriage? What is one thing you can do this week to build your marriage?

12. Gaining victory over selfishness is a lifelong process. A husband and wife need the guidance of God's Word. In the passage that follows, identify some building blocks that produce solid benefits in a home:

"By wisdom a house is built,
and through understanding it is established;
through knowledge its rooms are filled
with rare and beautiful treasures"
(Proverbs 24:3-4).

Scripture provides the wisdom, understanding, and knowledge that you need to build a marriage marked by oneness and harmony instead of isolation. The next six sessions of this study will explore the blueprints found in God's Word for building your home. Your discovery and application of these truths will result in a home that is built and filled with "rare and beautiful treasures"!

HomeBuilders Principle:
As you commit your life to God, deny yourself, and obey his Word, you can experience intimacy and build a God-honoring marriage.

W R A P • U P   15   M I N U T E S

The opposite of selfishness is self-denial, humility, and generosity. To close this session, you will have the opportunity to help your spouse. Take a minute to write down something that you will either do for your spouse or give up for your spouse during the next week. For example, you might choose to give up your normal Saturday activities and do something

To end this session, close with prayer following the Wrap-Up activity. You may want to have a closing corporate prayer, or close with spouses praying together. Be sure and Make a Date for the first HomeBuilders Project before leaving.

with your spouse. After writing this down, huddle with your spouse, and tell each other what you will do.

Make a Date

Make a date with your spouse to meet before the next session to complete the HomeBuilders Project for this session. Your leader will ask at the next session for you to share one insight or experience from your date.

DATE
_____

TIME
_____

LOCATION
_____

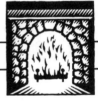

HOMEBUILDERS PROJECT   6 0   M I N U T E S

As a Couple [10 minutes]
Before working on this project, take a few minutes to talk with each other about your day by answering these questions:

- What was the best thing that happened to you today?

- What was the worst thing that happened?

- What was the funniest thing that happened?

Individually [20 minutes]

1. When have you felt especially close to your spouse?

2. What contributed to that closeness?

3. When has selfishness detracted from your closeness?

4. What would your marriage be like if you lived unselfishly? What changes would this require of you?

5. Read 1 Peter 3:8-12. Based on this passage, what are some things you should do when you believe your spouse is being selfish?

6. What is one thing you will do this week to show an unselfish attitude toward your spouse?

Interact as a Couple [30 minutes]
1. Share your discoveries from the previous questions.

2. No one enjoys hearing that he or she is being self-ish. Your marriage can benefit if you know how to best approach your spouse when you believe he or she is being selfish. Share a couple of ways you would like your spouse to help you deal with selfishness.

3. Together read the story Jesus told in Matthew 7:24-27, and discuss how you can relate this parable to building your marriage.

4. Close your date by praying for one another.

Remember to take your calendar to the next session for Make a Date.

Creating Oneness

Oneness in marriage is achieved as both husband and wife obey God and work together to build their home from the same set of blueprints: the Bible.

W A R M • U P   15   M I N U T E S

Dream House

Tear a blank sheet of paper in half. Individually, take two or three minutes to draw out a one-floor plan of what you would consider your "dream house"—the home you would love to build if you could. After you are finished, get with your spouse to compare floor plans and answer the following questions:

For this exercise, each couple will need one sheet of paper.

• In what ways are your floor plans similar?

• What are the biggest differences?

• How would you compare this exercise to marriage?

If a new couple joins the group, be sure to pass books around for couples to write their names, phone numbers, and e-mail addresses.

When each couple has had time to answer these questions, report to the group on your comparisons of the exercise to marriage.

Project Report

If you completed the HomeBuilders Project from the first session, share one thing you learned.

BLUEPRINTS   60 MINUTES

In the first session, we looked at how selfishness can produce isolation in marriage. In this session, we'll look at our need to work from the same set of blueprints as we seek to build a lasting marriage. Let's look at the Bible to learn about God's blueprints for replacing isolation with oneness.

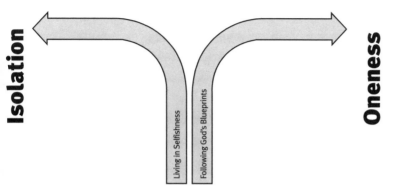

Living in selfishness leads to isolation, while following God's blueprints leads to oneness.

Benefits of Oneness

1. Read Psalm 133:1 and Ecclesiastes 4:9-12. What do these Scriptures say to you about some of the benefits of oneness in a relationship?

If you have a large group, you may want to break into smaller groups of about six people to answer the Blueprints questions. Unless otherwise noted, answer the questions in your subgroup. After finishing each section, take time for subgroups to share their answers with the whole group.

2. From your experience, what are some other benefits you gain from being one with your spouse?

Achieving Oneness

3. What is "oneness" in marriage?

4. What would society say are some ways to build oneness in marriage?

5. What is missing from most secular instruction about achieving oneness? How important are these missing elements? Why?

6. Read Philippians 2:1-2. Paul addresses the issue of oneness among Christians. How can you apply these principles to your marriage?

7. When is a time you and your spouse were not "like-minded" on an issue? What was the result?

> **HomeBuilders Principle:**
> *Oneness in your marriage involves complete unity with each other.*

God's Purposes for Marriage

8. Have each couple choose one of the following verses. (It's OK for the same verse to be selected more than once if more than three couples are in the group.)

- Genesis 1:27
- Genesis 1:28
- Genesis 2:18

Read your verse, and discuss how it relates to God's purposes for marriage. Then take turns sharing with the group your verse and insights into God's purposes for marriage.

> **HomeBuilders Principle:**
> *To achieve oneness, you must share a strong commitment to God's purposes for marriage.*

9. What can you apply to your marriage from the verses that you just discussed?

10. How well does your marriage reflect God's image and model his attributes to others? As a couple, give yourselves a rating from one (low) to ten (high) in the areas and relationships that follow. Also jot down some ways you can demonstrate these traits.

We reflect God's...	to each other	to our families	to others
...perfect love for imperfect people;			
...loving-kindness, by serving to meet needs;			
...commit-ment, by patient support;			
...peace, by resolving conflicts.			

Evaluate with your spouse the areas in which you were strongest and those that need the most improvement. What are one or two steps you can take to better reflect God's image and model his attributes in your marriage?

11. Share with the whole group one discovery from the previous exercise.

W R A P • U P   15   M I N U T E S

Form a group with two other couples. Share with this group something you really appreciate about your spouse. After everyone has spoken, go around the group a second time if you would like. Then take prayer requests, and close with a time of prayer in your group.

Make a Date

Make a date with your spouse to meet before the next session to complete the HomeBuilders Project for this session. Your leader will ask at the next session for you to share one insight or experience from your date.

DATE

TIME

LOCATION

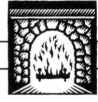

HOMEBUILDERS PROJECT   6 o   M I N U T E S

As a Couple [10 minutes]
Start your date by taking a short walk together. As you walk, reminisce about the places you would walk together when you were dating.

Individually [20 minutes]
1. What would you say is the purpose of your marriage?

2. What might your closest friend say is the purpose of your marriage, based on his or her observations?

3. In what aspects of oneness do you think your marriage is succeeding?

4. What aspects of oneness need work in your marriage?

5. How "like-minded" are you and your spouse on the values and goals in your marriage? Rate that aspect of your relationship on a scale of one (low) to ten (high).

6. What are some things that you can do to promote oneness in your marriage?

Interact as a Couple [30 minutes]

1. Discuss your answers to the previous questions.

2. Agree on any action steps you should take and how they will be implemented.

3. Close your time together by praying for one another and for your success in following God's blueprints for marriage.

Remember to take your calendar to the next session for Make a Date.

Receiving Your Spouse

Oneness in marriage requires receiving your spouse
as God's perfect provision for your needs.

W A R M • U P   15   M I N U T E S

"What I Like, How About You?"

In each of the following six categories, how do you
see yourself? How do you see your spouse? How does
your spouse see you? On the spectrum lines for each
category, place a Y where you see yourself and an S
where you see your spouse. When you're finished,
compare your results with your spouse's! Then share
with the group the one category in which your ratings
most closely agreed or disagreed.

• MUSIC

A little bit country _____ A little bit rock 'n' roll

• MOVIES

Comedy ───────────────────────── Drama

(categories continued on next page)

• NUTRITION

Health ————————————————————————————— Junk
food   food

• FINANCES

"You can't take ———————————————————— "A penny saved is
it with you."   a penny earned."

• VACATION

Go, go, go ———————————————————————— Slow down,
                                                       relax

• TECHNOLOGY

Wired ———————————————————————————— Off-line

Project Report

Share one thing you learned from the HomeBuilders
Project from last session.

BLUEPRINTS   60 MINUTES

We have seen that selfishness produces isolation in
marriage, and following God's blueprints leads to oneness. Now let's study the importance of receiving your
spouse as God's special gift to you.

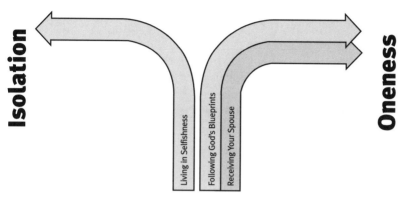

Receiving your spouse as God's gift to you helps create oneness in marriage.

In Genesis 2:18-24, we find the familiar story of Adam and Eve. Our familiarity with Scriptures such as this can blind us to profound insights. Let's look at what we can learn from this passage to help us to fully accept our spouse as God's provision.

Our Need for a Spouse

Read Genesis 2:18-20.

1. What need did God build into Adam? How do we share that need?

2. Why do you think God created Adam with the need for a helper?

God's Provision for Our Need

Read Genesis 2:21-22.

3. How did God go about creating Eve? Be specific.

4. Why do you suppose God chose to create Eve this way?

Our Response to God's Provision

Read Genesis 2:23-24.

5. How do you think Adam felt when he first saw Eve?

6. How were Adam and Eve able to recognize they were made for each other?

HomeBuilders Principle:
You can fully accept your spouse because of faith in God's character and trustworthiness.

You and Your Spouse

7. In what ways does modern culture encourage you to be independent of your spouse?

If you have a large group, you may want to break into smaller groups of about six people to answer questions 7 through 9. After answering these questions, take time for subgroups to share their answers with the whole group.

8. What are some things that cause people to reject rather than accept their spouses?

9. Consider the results of not receiving your spouse. What have you observed in the relationships of married couples who do not accept each other as God's provision for their needs?

10. If you truly receive your spouse as God's provision for you, how can that affect your attitude toward your spouse's weaknesses?

Answer questions 11 and 12 with your spouse. After answering, you may want to share an appropriate insight or discovery with the group.

11. What are some ways you need your spouse? In what ways has this changed since you were first married?

12. What are some differences in your spouse that God uses to complement you?

HomeBuilders Principle:
A God-honoring marriage is not created by finding a flawless spouse, but by allowing God's perfect love and acceptance to flow through an imperfect person — you — toward another imperfect person — your mate.

Individually write down as many ways as you can think of in one minute that your spouse has helped you during the last week. When time is up, exchange lists with your spouse. Everyone should then share with the group one thing from the list they received.

For Extra Impact

Each couple in the group should have a common household tool that has two parts (like a pair of scissors, a manual can opener, or a pair of pliers). Take a minute to study your tool. Note any observations you have, specifically its function, how it works, and what makes it unique. Then as a group discuss the following questions:

Tools: For an active illustration of the need for oneness in marriage, do this exercise.

• What observations did you make?

• How would you compare marriage to these tools?

Make a Date

Make a date with your spouse to meet before the next session to complete the HomeBuilders Project. Your leader will ask you to share something from this experience at the next session.

DATE

TIME

LOCATION

HOMEBUILDERS PROJECT   6 0   M I N U T E S

As a Couple [5 minutes]
To start your date, pull out your wedding album, and take a few minutes to relive your wedding day. As you look at the pictures, talk about the way you felt at that moment.

Individually [30 minutes]
This project is a special one—writing a love letter to your spouse. You'll write this letter on a separate sheet of paper using the questions under "Love

Letter" as an outline. But before starting your letter, spend five or ten minutes in private prayer using the following questions to guide your prayer time.

Prayer Time

1. Confess to God as sin any rejection of, withdrawal from, or bitterness toward your spouse. Thank God for his forgiveness and the cleansing blood of Christ.

"If we confess our sins,
he is faithful and just and will forgive us our
sins and purify us from all unrighteousness"
(1 John 1:9).

2. Commit to God totally, by faith, to receive your spouse based upon the integrity and sovereignty of God. Be sure to put this commitment in your love letter.

3. Commit to God to trust him with your spouse's weaknesses and to love your spouse unconditionally with Christ's love (apart from performance). Be certain you put this commitment in your love letter.

Love Letter

1. What were the qualities that most attracted me to you when we first met?

2. Do I see and accept you as you really are? What have I not accepted in you?

3. Do you see and accept me as I really am? In what areas do I believe that you have not accepted me? How does this make me feel?

Interact as a Couple [25 minutes]
1. Exchange letters. (You may want to read the letter you receive aloud, or your spouse may want to read his or her letter to you.)

2. Discuss what you learned from the letters.

3. Tell your spouse about the commitment you made to God during your prayer time.

4. Pray together. Take turns thanking God for each other.

Remember to take your calendar to the next session for Make a Date.

Constructing a Relationship

Building your marriage involves a process of leaving parents, uniting with each other, and becoming one.

W A R M • U P   15   M I N U T E S

A Match Made in Paradise

In separate groups of men and women, come up with lists of things you think made Adam and Eve's marriage good. For example, "They didn't have to face the dilemma of whose family to visit during the next holiday." Have fun with this activity.

After a few minutes, come back together, share your lists, and answer the following questions:

• In what ways are the lists similar?

- How are they different?

- What discoveries did you make in your discussion?

Project Report

Share something with the group that you found significant in doing the "Love Letter" assignment from last session.

BLUEPRINTS   6 o MINUTES

In the last session, we looked at how we can receive our spouse as God's provision for our needs. In this session we will examine the phases that are involved in constructing a marriage relationship.

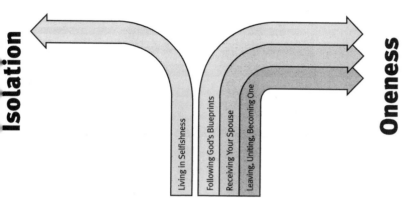

God's plan for oneness includes the process of leaving, uniting, and becoming one.

God's plan for the lifelong process of constructing a
God-honoring marriage has three practical phases. In
one short verse in Genesis, we find these three phases:

> *"For this reason a man will leave*
> *his father and mother and be united to his wife,*
> *and they will become one flesh"*
> (Genesis 2:24).

A common error in marriage relationships is the
assumption that these phases have already been
fulfilled. Many people think the command to leave
parents, unite, and become one flesh is only for

newlyweds. This session will show how each phase involves a lifelong process of achieving and maintaining a relationship of openness and trust.

Phase One: Leaving

Break into groups of about six people. If you have six or fewer, remain in one group. In your group, read aloud the following Case Study, choosing a reader for each of the three parts (Narrator, Craig, and Karen). After reading the Case Study, answer the questions. Then elect a spokesperson to report your answers to the whole group.

Case Study

Narrator: After several years of apartment living, Craig and Karen bought their first home. And it happened just in time—their second child was due only two months after the closing date. Their purchase was a beautiful, four-bedroom home in a new subdivision. The price had been a little beyond their means, but both Craig's parents and Karen's parents had given them some money to use toward the down payment.

Craig was happy with their new home until he received some startling news after they moved in. Karen's parents, who lived in the same town, had decided to sell the home they had owned for twenty-five years and were going to move to a house across the street! Karen seemed thrilled. Craig was not. He thought Karen's mother had a controlling personality, but Karen had a difficult time understanding his concern.

Karen: They were lonely in that old house. Now we can see them more often, and Mom can help with the kids.

Craig: But you see them almost every day anyway! You know how much I like your parents, but we've got to have a life of our own. With them here it will be like they're still in charge of our lives. Your mom will be over here telling us how to raise our kids.

Karen: Mom does nothing but help us week after week. Why, just last weekend you didn't have any problem with her baby-sitting our son while we went on a date.

Craig: Yes, and I also had to listen to her for fifteen minutes telling me all the things I was doing wrong with Tommy. You'd think she never made any mistakes when she was our age.

Karen: She's a parent, Craig. They can't stop giving advice just because we've left home. We'll be doing the same thing when we're older. Besides, I don't see you speaking up when your own father puts pressure on you to spend Christmas with them every year.

Craig: That's totally different.

Karen: No, it's not. You say we need to live our own lives. Have you told your parents that? Have you stood up to them when they try to manipulate us and make us feel guilty just because we want to start our own traditions for the holidays?

Craig: You know how hard it is to stand up to my dad.

Karen: Yes I do, and that's my point. If we're going to talk about "living our own lives," let's step back and look at everything— not just my parents.

1. What are some mistakes the people in this story are making?

2. What do you think Craig and Karen's next step should be?

3. What happens in a marriage relationship when:
- Parents are too clingy?

- A spouse is more dependent on parents than his or her mate?

4. Ephesians 6:2 says, "Honor your father and mother." How can you be separate from your parents and still honor them?

Phase Two: Uniting

Answer question 5 in your subgroup. After answering this question, each group should share its response.

5. In Genesis 2:24, what does "be united to his wife" mean? What is the relationship between leaving your parents and being united to your spouse?

6. What was one of the first difficult chal-
lenges to your commitment to each other that
you faced early in your marriage?

Answer questions 6 and
7 with your spouse. After
answering, you may want
to share an appropriate
insight or discovery with
the entire group.

7. How did that challenge affect your commitment to
each other?

Phase Three: Becoming One

8. The third step in constructing a God-
honoring marriage is to "become one
flesh"—to establish physical intimacy. Why
is becoming one flesh important in achieving oneness in marriage?

Answer question 8 in
your subgroup, then
groups should report
their answers.

9. List two or three of the most romantic times you've
had with your spouse. Then share lists with your spouse.

The Result: Naked and Unashamed

10. Genesis 2:25 tells us, "The man and his wife were both naked, and they felt no shame." What is the significance of this? How is this a picture of oneness?

W R A P • U P   15   M I N U T E S

As a couple, pick one of the following three questions to answer. Then share your answer with the group.

- Leaving: What is one area in which you have a healthy separation from your parents?

- Uniting: What is one experience you've been through lately that has drawn you closer together?

- Becoming One: What is one really romantic date you've had as a couple? (You may want to look at question 9 in Blueprints.)

Make a Date

Make a date with your spouse to meet before the next session to complete the HomeBuilders Project. Your leader will ask at the next session for you to share one thing from this experience.

DATE

TIME

LOCATION

HOMEBUILDERS PROJECT   6 0   M I N U T E S

As a Couple [10 minutes]

Plan a special date. Talk about a place you would like to go or something you would like to do. Discuss things you could do to help make this date romantic. To help generate some ideas, you may want to think back to some previous special times and recall what details helped make those occasions memorable.

Individually [25 minutes]

Leaving

1. Use the following chart to rank yourself in each area of leaving your parents.

1 - No dependence on parents
2 - Some dependence on parents
3 - Neutral
4 - Strong dependence on parents
5 - Total dependence on parents

1	2	3	4	5	Financial Dependence
1	2	3	4	5	Social Dependence
1	2	3	4	5	Emotional Dependence
1	2	3	4	5	Acceptance and Approval

2. What area of "leaving parents" do you need to work on the most? What are some ways you can do this?

Uniting

3. Answer the following questions either Y (yes) or N (no).

Y N   I have not threatened to leave my spouse within the past two years.

Y N   My spouse is secure in my commitment to our marriage.

Y N   I am more committed to my spouse than to my career.

Y N   My spouse knows I am more committed to our marriage than to my career.

Y N   I am more committed to my spouse than to my friends and hobbies.

Y N   I don't withdraw emotionally from my spouse for an extended period of time following a conflict.

Y N   I generally do not leave my spouse mentally by staying preoccupied with other things.

Y N   I am interested in my spouse's needs and actively do what I can to meet them.

4. Review your answers, and determine some ways you can demonstrate a stronger commitment to your spouse.

5. If there are some specific areas from this exercise for which you need to ask your spouse's forgiveness, list them.

6. What setting makes it easy for you to share intimately with your spouse?

7. How could the two of you improve the intimacy you share?

8. What do you most enjoy about your sex life?

9. In what ways other than physically are you one with your spouse?

Interact as a Couple [25 minutes]

1. Review the "Leaving" exercise chart and question.

2. Share your answers to questions 4 and 5 from the "Uniting" exercise.

3. Share with each other your answers to all of the "Becoming One" questions.

4. Work together to identify one or two actions for you to take in the coming week in response to your discussion.

5. End your date by praying together.

Remember to take your calendar to the next session for Make a Date.

Fitting Together

God wants husbands and wives to assume biblical responsibilities within their marriages.

W A R M • U P   15   M I N U T E S

"Please Pass the Roles"

Read the following list of household chores, and assign an M to each task you regularly perform, an S to each chore your spouse usually does, or a B to the tasks that you share. If a task is listed that doesn't apply, place the letter X next to it.

__ take out the trash

__ make the bed

__ prepare dinner

__ clean out the garage

__ hang wallpaper

__ maintain the vehicle(s)

__ wash dishes

__ run errands (such as to the bank, post office, or cleaners)

__ do the laundry

__ mow the lawn

__ clean bathrooms

__ pay the bills

__ make general household repairs

__ shop for groceries

__ vacuum

__ paint the house (interior)

(list continued on p. 60)

__ dust	__ clear the table
__ paint the house (exterior)	__ drive (when you're in the car together)

After everyone has finished assigning the appropriate letters, answer the following questions:

- What was the total number of tasks to which you assigned the letter M? How about B?

- Within this group what, if any, chores were exclusively done by men or women? Why do you think this is? How do you feel about that?

- What does this exercise tell you about marriage?

Project Report

Share one discovery you made from last session's HomeBuilders Project.

Oneness results when a couple follows God's blueprints, accepts one another as God's gift, and then constructs their marriage by leaving parents, uniting with each other, and becoming one. In this session, you will study patterns that are essential in becoming God-honoring husbands and wives. Only as we understand the roles God has given to us can we obtain oneness in marriage.

For Blueprints in this session you will be in two groups—one for husbands and one for wives. Blueprints for husbands start on page 62 and for wives on page 65.

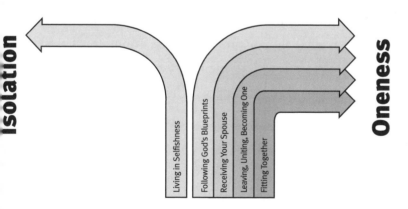

A part of oneness involves fitting together—fulfilling your biblical responsibilities as husbands and wives.

A Special Note: This session deals with "core roles," not comprehensive lifestyles or specific tasks. These responsibilities are never presented as describing the totality of a person's life, but as a central focus around which a person may build varied interests and involvements. All other forms of employment, recreation, and ministry will naturally vary in intensity and importance in different individuals and at different stages of life.

Blueprints for Husbands

It will not be possible in this session to cover all of the questions that could be raised about the roles of husbands and wives. Our goal is to help you develop a biblical job description as a husband by focusing on what the Bible says.

Marriage Today

1. In our culture, many voices are telling men and women what they ought to be like. What are these cultural voices telling men they need to be in order to be successful in marriage? What are women told?

2. In what ways have marital roles changed during the last few decades? How have these changes strengthened marriages? How have they weakened marriages?

Biblical Responsibilities

3. Read Ephesians 5:21-33. What is your initial reaction to this passage?

4. What standards do you see husbands being given in this passage? What standards are given to wives? How do you feel about those standards?

5. Why do you think Paul repeatedly instructs husbands to love their wives in this passage? What does it mean for a husband to love his wife "as Christ loved the church"? How would this kind of love affect your marriage?

6. What do you think Ephesians 5:23 means when it calls Christ "the head of the church"? How should Christ's headship compare to the husband being "the head of the wife"?

7. With Christ as our example, how do the following passages relate to you as a husband?
- Mark 10:42-45

- John 13:1-5; 12-17

- John 15:12-13

- 1 Corinthians 13:4-7

- 1 John 3:16-18

8. In your home, do you tend to be more passive or more dictatorial? With Christ as the model, what should be your goal?

9. Based on what you have studied and discussed, write a biblical job description for you as a husband, and then share it with the other men.

HomeBuilders Principle for Husbands:
To honor God in your marriage, you need to provide servant-leadership and to love your wife as Christ loves the church.

Blueprints for Wives

It will not be possible in this session to cover all of the questions that could be raised about the roles of husbands and wives. Our goal is to help you develop a biblical job description as a wife by focusing on what the Bible says.

Marriage Today

1. In our culture, many voices are telling men and women what they ought to be like. What are these cultural voices telling women they need to be in order to be successful in marriage? What are men told?

2. In what ways have marital roles changed during the last few decades? How have these changes strengthened marriages? How have they weakened marriages?

Biblical Responsibilities

3. Read Ephesians 5:21-33. What standards do you see wives being given in this passage? What standards are given to husbands? How do you feel about those standards?

4. What do you think Ephesians 5:23 means when it says, "For the husband is the head of the wife"? Why do you think Paul addresses this statement to wives?

5. If your husband truly loved you "as Christ loved the church," what effect would it have on your marriage?

6. How would it affect your marriage if you were to "submit to your husband as to the Lord"?

7. Ephesians 5:33b says "the wife must respect her husband." What do you think this means? What does "respect" look like?

8. Read the following Scriptures. How do these verses relate to you as a wife?
   • Proverbs 31:10-31

- 1 Corinthians 11:11-12

- Galatians 3:26-29

- Titus 2:1-5

- 1 Peter 3:1-6

9. Based on what you have studied and discussed, write a biblical job description for you as a wife, and then share it with the other women.

HomeBuilders Principle for Wives:
To honor God in your marriage, you need to love your husband, respect him, and support him.

Get with your spouse, and share the job description you wrote during Blueprints. After sharing, answer this question together: What are some ways you can fulfill your job description during the next week?

Make a Date

Make a date with your spouse to meet before the next session to complete the HomeBuilders Project. Your leader will ask at the next session for you to share one thing from this experience.

_____

DATE

_____

TIME

_____

LOCATION

As a Couple [10 minutes]

Take a minute to reminisce about the chores you had to do when you were a kid. Which of these was your least favorite? Why?

Revisit the list of chores in the Warm-Up section of this session, and answer these questions:

- How have the chores you do now changed from when you were first married?

- Which task are you most grateful that your spouse does?

Individually [20 minutes]

1. Start by taking a minute to pray. Ask God to show you how you can be the best possible spouse for your mate.

2. In general, how do you feel about the roles you and your spouse currently fill in your marriage relationship?

3. In what ways has this session challenged the way you think about your responsibilities in your marriage?

4. What is a specific responsibility you need to take to show true love to your spouse?

5. What is a responsibility your spouse fills that you really appreciate? How can you show your appreciation for this?

6. What do you believe is the most important role or responsibility you have in your marriage?

Interact as a Couple [30 minutes]

1. Share and discuss your answers to the previous questions.

2. From your discussion, what is one insight you have gained about your spouse?

3. What are some specific ways you can support and encourage each other as you carry out your roles as husband and wife?

4. Close your date by praying together. Thank God for one another, and ask for his help in meeting the commitments you've made.

Remember to take your calendar to the next session for Make a Date.

Building in the Spirit

A husband and wife can experience true oneness only as they live by faith, in the power of the Holy Spirit.

W A R M • U P   15   M I N U T E S

The Moral of the Story

Think back to the childhood tale of "The Three Little Pigs." What is the moral of the story? Now read Jesus' story of the wise and foolish builders (Matthew 7:24-27).

- What is similar in the two stories? What is the key difference in the conclusion of each story?

- In relation to marriage, what are some of the foundations on which people build?

• On what foundation does a "wise" couple build?

Project Report

Share one thing you learned from the HomeBuilders
Project from last session.

For Extra Impact

Bouncing Balloons:
To see the need for help in living a God-honoring marriage, do this exercise. You will need two uninflated balloons and a marker for each couple.

Pass around balloons and markers. Every couple should have two uninflated balloons and a marker. Blow up and tie your balloon, then write on your balloon as many of the practical things you have learned during the past five sessions as you can. Once everyone's balloons are ready, toss them into the air in the middle of the group. As a group, try to keep all of the balloons in the air for as long as you can. You may want to keep time to see how long you can make it. Try this a couple times to see if you can improve on your time. When you've finished, pick up the balloon closest to you, and answer these questions:

• What does the balloon you are holding say?

• How easy was it to keep all the balloons up?

• How easy do you find it to do everything you know you should in your marriage? Why?

For a home to weather the storms of life, its daily builder must be God. Jesus said it was to our advantage that he go to the Father, because he would send God's Holy Spirit (the "Helper" or "Comforter," the Third Person of the Trinity) to lead us, show us his ways, and to empower us to represent him to the world. (See John 14:26.) As two people build a relationship with each other, it is essential that they both yield to the Holy Spirit and allow him to lead them in every facet of their marriage.

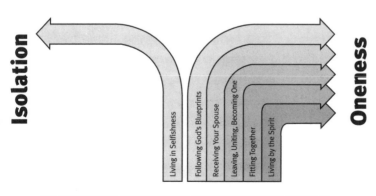

In order to be fully one, a husband and wife should each commit to live by the Spirit.

The House That Human Nature Builds

If you have a large group, break into smaller groups of about six people to answer the Blueprints questions. Unless otherwise noted, answer the questions in your subgroup. After finishing each section, take time for subgroups to share their answers with the whole group.

1. Read Romans 7:18-19. Why do you think it is a struggle at times to do the right thing?

2. Read Galatians 5:16-21. What effects can your own desires and effort ("the acts of the sinful nature") have on your marriage relationship?

3. Read 1 Corinthians 2:14–3:3. What kind of people do you see being described in these verses? Which description best fits you?

4. Why might a "spiritual" person still act "worldly"? What is the remedy?

The House the Spirit Builds

5. You have read "the acts of the sinful nature" (Galatians 5:19-21); now look at "the fruit of the

Spirit." Read Galatians 5:22-26. What are the characteristics of a person who is living by the Spirit?

6. Why do you think it is important for the Holy Spirit to be present within a marriage?

7. From verses 22 and 23 of Galatians 5, what specific fruit of the Spirit do you need more of to improve the oneness in your marriage? Explain.

Answer questions 7 and 8 with your spouse. After answering, you may want to share an appropriate insight or discovery with the group.

8. What specific fruit of the Spirit do you see most evident in the life of your spouse?

HomeBuilders Principle:
Only through the Holy Spirit can you build a God-honoring home.

The Holy Spirit in Your Life

9. The Holy Spirit plays many roles in the life of a Christian. Each couple should choose one of the passages that follow. (It's OK for a couple to take more than one passage or for more than one couple to have the same passage.)

- John 14:26
- John 16:13
- Romans 8:16
- John 16:8
- Acts 1:8
- Romans 8:26

Read your passage, and discuss the work of the Holy Spirit it reveals. Take turns sharing with the group your verse and its insight into the ministry of the Holy Spirit.

10. In what ways can the Holy Spirit help you build your marriage?

HomeBuilders Principle:
The home built by God requires both you and your spouse to give control of your lives to the Holy Spirit.

If you would like the power of the Holy Spirit in your life and your marriage, give control of your life to Christ. Confess your sins, and let Christ take over. To live consistently in the power of the Holy Spirit, you need to make certain daily that you are living under God's control.

End the session with a time of prayer. Say the following prayer if it reflects the desire of your heart:

Dear God, I need you. I acknowledge that I have been in control of my life and that, as a result, I have sinned against you. I thank you that you have forgiven my sins through Christ's death on the cross for me. I now ask you to again take control of my life. Empower and guide me through your Holy Spirit. As an expression of my faith, I now thank you for taking control of my life through the Holy Spirit. I pray this in Jesus' name, amen.

Make a Date

Make a date with your spouse to meet before the next

session to complete the HomeBuilders Project. Your
leader will ask at the next session for you to share
one thing from this experience.

DATE
_____

TIME
_____

LOCATION
_____

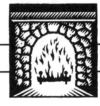

HOMEBUILDERS PROJECT   6 0   M I N U T E S

As a Couple [10 minutes]
Share with one another about your spiritual journey
by answering a couple of the following questions.

• Who in your life has had the greatest spiritual
  impact on you? In what way?

• What Bible story, passage, or verse means a lot
  to you?

• What is one of your earliest memories of church?

Individually [25 minutes]

1. What is one insight you have gained about the Holy Spirit from this session?

2. What is one practical way you can apply what you learned in your life this week?

3. In what ways does the Holy Spirit help you in your life?

4. Where in your life do you need the power of the Holy Spirit the most right now?

5. What in your life might be hindering the work of the Holy Spirit?

6. Confess to God any sin that might be hindering his work in your life, and ask him to help you walk in the Spirit.

Interact as a Couple [25 minutes]
1. Share with one another from the previous questions. Your relationship will benefit from an open discussion about spiritual things—as well as confiding questions or struggles you may have. (Caution: Be forgiving if your spouse reveals a disconcerting struggle.)

2. How can you help and encourage each other to walk in the power of the Holy Spirit?

3. In what practical, everyday situations could the power of the Holy Spirit make a difference in your marriage?

4. Close your time together by praying for one another.

Remember to take your calendar to the next session for Make a Date.

There is a "For Extra Impact" exercise on the next page.

For Extra Impact

For God's Eyes Only: You may want to do this exercise as part of your personal quiet time this week.

An exercise that many Christians have found meaningful is to take a separate sheet of paper and spend time alone with God, asking him to reveal any sin that is unconfessed before him. The following steps are recommended:

1. Title the page "For God's Eyes Only." Prayerfully list on the page actions and attitudes that are contrary to God's Word and purposes. Focus on areas that affect your spouse.

2. After a time of self-examination, write the words of 1 John 1:9 across your list of sins, thanking God for his absolute forgiveness of all that you have done in the past, present, and future.

3. Thank him for sending his Son to the cross to die for your sin.

4. It may be necessary and appropriate for you to also confess to your spouse any attitudes or actions that have been harmful to him or her. Caution: If you are unsure about the appropriateness of sharing something, seek wise counsel.

5. Destroy the page.

6. Bow in prayer, and acknowledge God's authority over your life.

Building a Legacy

Building a God-honoring legacy requires that you determine together to influence your world and future generations for Christ.

W A R M • U P   15   M I N U T E S

Lasting Legacy

Our lives have been shaped by the influence of others. Look over the following list of skills, and think about who taught you each skill. Pick one thing from the list, and share with the group who taught you the skill. You may also want to tell about something else important this person passed on to you.

- Bait a fishing hook
- Tie shoelaces
- Pray
- Work
- Say "please" and "thank you"

- Drive a car
- Be a good sport
- Throw a ball
- Cook
- Read

Project Report

Share one insight or discovery from last session's
HomeBuilders Project.

BLUEPRINTS   60 MINUTES

You have studied that oneness with God and with
your spouse is necessary for overcoming isolation in
marriage. This oneness you are establishing in your
home also enables you to reach out to others.

God's heart of love is virtually breaking over people
who have not yet received his forgiveness through his
Son, Jesus Christ. Reconciling people to himself is
God's desire for every individual. You and your
spouse and those you influence for Christ, including
your children, are all a part of God's purpose.

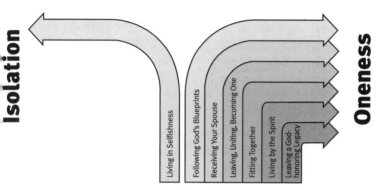

Isolation ← → Oneness

Living in Selfishness
Following God's Blueprints
Receiving Your Spouse
Leaving, Uniting, Becoming One
Fitting Together
Living by the Spirit
Leaving a God-honoring Legacy

The oneness you establish as a couple allows you to impact others in a God-honoring way with your lives.

Married people who work together to meet needs beyond their own front door will leave a spiritual legacy that will outlive them. The legacy left will ultimately be different for everyone. The true test in leaving a God-honoring legacy is an individual's or a couple's faithful fulfillment of God's mission through the stewardship of time, talents, and treasure. A God-honoring legacy can be partially measured in the character of the descendants who have been spiritually influenced by a person's life.

If you have a large group, break into smaller groups of about six people to answer the Blueprints questions. Unless otherwise noted, answer the questions in your subgroup. After finishing each section, take time for subgroups to share their answers with the whole group.

Understanding Our Legacy

1. When you think of a "heritage" or a "legacy," what comes to mind?

2. What are some other types of legacies people leave? List as many different kinds as you can.

3. What kind of legacy have your parents left you? How do you feel about this legacy?

4. As couples, look up one of the following Scriptures. (Depending on the number of couples in the group, it's OK for a couple to take more than one passage, or to have more than one couple take the same passage.)

- Joshua 24:14-15

- Psalm 112:1-2

- 2 Timothy 1:5

- 3 John 4

Read your passage together, and jot down words, thoughts, or phrases you believe describe the legacy God desires you to leave. Then share your Scripture and what you wrote with the whole group.

> **HomeBuilders Principle:**
> *The legacy you were handed is not as important as the legacy you will leave.*

Leaving a Legacy Beyond Yourself

5. What do 2 Timothy 2:2 and Matthew 28:19-20 say about leaving a spiritual legacy?

6. According to Deuteronomy 6:4-9, how do you leave a God-honoring legacy through your influence on your children?

HomeBuilders Principle:
The legacy you leave is determined by the life you live.

Motivation for Leaving a God-Honoring Legacy

7. For this question, break into three groups (a group can be one couple). Each group will take one of the Scripture passages that follow:

- Romans 8:31-39
- 1 Peter 3:9-16
- 2 Peter 3:8-15

Read your passage in your group, and answer this question: What in the verses you read motivates you to leave a God-honoring legacy? After groups have had time to answer, come back together, and share answers.

8. Read 1 Corinthians 3:10-15, and contrast the final results of a worldly and God-honoring legacy.

9. What would your legacy be if it were based only on your life up through today?

Answer questions 9 and 10 with your spouse. After answering, you may want to share an appropriate insight or discovery with the group.

10. What do you want your legacy to be? What people might God want you to influence?

W R A P • U P   15 M I N U T E S

As you come to the end of this study, take some time to reflect as a group on what you have experienced. Pick one of the following questions to answer and share with the group.

- What has this group meant to you during the course of this study? Be specific.

- What is the most valuable thing you discovered?

- What would you like to see happen next for this group?

• How have you changed?

Make a Date

Make a date with your spouse to meet in the next few days to complete the last HomeBuilders Project of this study.

DATE

TIME

LOCATION

HOMEBUILDERS PROJECT   6 o   M I N U T E S

As a Couple [10 minutes]
Congratulations—you've made it to the last project for this study. To start this date, reflect on the effect this study has had on your marriage by answering the following questions:

- Think back to the first meeting of this study. How did you feel? What expectations did you have? How did your experience compare to your expectations?

- What is something from this study that has helped your marriage?

- What is something you learned about your spouse?

- What has been the best part of this study for you?

Individually [20 minutes]

1. Write a description of the legacy you desire to leave:
- to your physical descendants—your children, if God so blesses.

- to your spiritual descendants—those you influence for Chirst through mentoring and discipleship.

2. What is one major objective you wish to accomplish this year to help you:

- leave a God-honoring line of physical descendants.

- leave a God-honoring line of spiritual descendants.

Interact as a Couple [30 minutes]

1. Compare the legacy descriptions you wrote, then write one common description of the legacy you both desire to leave (you may want to copy or type this description and place it somewhere at home or work as a reminder):

- for your physical descendants.

- for your spiritual descendants.

2. What is one specific action you can agree to take together to help your marriage leave a God-honoring legacy? (For some ideas, see page 99.)

3. Beyond this study, what can you do as a couple to continue regularly setting some time aside to build your marriage?

4. Close with a time of prayer, thanking God for one another and for your marriage—what he has done and will do!

Please visit our Web site at www.familylife.com/homebuilders to give us your feedback on this study and to get information on other FamilyLife resources and conferences.

Where Do You Go From Here?

It is our prayer that you have benefited greatly from this study in the HomeBuilders Couples Series. We hope that your marriage will continue to grow as you both submit your lives to Jesus Christ and build according to his blueprints.

We also hope that you will begin reaching out to strengthen other marriages in your community and local church. Your church needs couples like you who are committed to building Christian marriages. A favorite World War II story illustrates this point very clearly.

The year was 1940. The French Army had just collapsed under Hitler's onslaught. The Dutch had folded, overwhelmed by the Nazi regime. The Belgians had surrendered. And the British Army was trapped on the coast of France in the channel port of Dunkirk.

Two hundred twenty thousand of Britain's finest young men seemed doomed to die, turning the English Channel red with their blood. The Fuehrer's troops, only miles away in the hills of France, didn't realize how close to victory they actually were.

Any rescue seemed feeble and futile in the time remaining. A "thin" British Navy—"the professionals"—told King George VI that at best they could save seventeen thousand troops. The House of Commons was warned to prepare for "hard and heavy tidings."

Politicians were paralyzed. The king was powerless. And the Allies could only watch as spectators from a distance. Then as the doom of the British Army seemed imminent, a strange fleet appeared on the horizon of the English Channel—the wildest assortment of boats perhaps ever assembled in history.

Trawlers, tugs, scows, fishing sloops, lifeboats, pleasure craft, smacks and coasters, sailboats, even the London fire-brigade flotilla. *Each ship was manned by civilian volunteers—English fathers sailing to rescue Britain's exhausted, bleeding sons.*

William Manchester writes in his epic novel *The Last Lion* that even today what happened in 1940 in less than twenty-four hours seems like a miracle—not only were all of the British soldiers rescued, but 118,000 other Allied troops as well.

Today the Christian home is much like those troops at Dunkirk. Pressured, trapped, and demoralized, it needs help. Your help. The Christian community may be much like England—we stand waiting for politicians, professionals, even for our pastors to step in and save the family. But the problem is much larger than all of those combined can solve.

With the highest divorce rate of any nation on earth, we need an all-out effort by men and women "sailing" to rescue the exhausted and wounded family casualties. We need an outreach effort by common couples with faith in an uncommon God. For too long, married couples within the church have abdicated the privilege and responsibility of influencing others to those in full-time vocational ministry.

Possibly this study has indeed been used to "light the torch" of your spiritual lives. Perhaps it was already burning, and this provided more fuel. Regardless, may we challenge you to invest your lives in others?

You and other couples around the world can team together to build thousands of marriages and families. By starting a HomeBuilders group, you will not only strengthen other marriages; you will also see your marriage grow as you share these principles with others.

Will You Join Us in "Touching Lives...Changing Families"?

The following are some practical ways you can make a difference in families today:

1. Gather a group of four to seven couples, and lead them through the seven sessions of this HomeBuilders study, *Building Your Marriage*. (Why not consider challenging others in your church or community to form additional HomeBuilders groups?)

2. Commit to continue marriage building by doing another small-group study in the HomeBuilders Couples Series.

3. An excellent outreach tool is the film "*JESUS*," which is available on video. For more information, contact Family Life at 1-800-FL-TODAY.

4. Host a dinner party. Invite families from your neighborhood to your home, and as a couple share your faith in Christ.

5. Reach out and share the love of Christ with neighborhood children.

6. If you have attended the FamilyLife Marriage Conference, why not offer to assist your pastor in counseling couples engaged to be married using the material you received?

For more information about any of the above ministry opportunities, contact your local church, or write:

FamilyLife
P.O. Box 8220
Little Rock, AR 72221-8220
1-800-FL-TODAY
www.familylife.com

Our Problems, God's Answers

—————————————•—————————————

Every couple eventually has to deal with problems in marriage. Communication problems. Money problems. Difficulties with sexual intimacy. These issues are important to cultivating a strong, loving relationship with your spouse. The HomeBuilders Couples Series is designed to help you strengthen your marriage in many of these critical areas.

Part One: The Big Problem

One basic problem is at the heart of every other problem in every marriage, and it's a problem we can't help you fix. No matter how hard you try, this is one problem that is too big for you to deal with on your own.

The problem is separation from God. If you want to experience marriage the way it was designed to be, you need a vital relationship with the God who created you and offers you the power to live a life of joy and purpose.

And what separates us from God is one more problem—sin. Most of us have assumed throughout our lives that the term "sin" refers to a list of bad habits that everyone agrees are wrong. We try to deal with our sin problem by working hard to become better people. We read books to learn how to control our anger, or we resolve to stop cheating on our taxes.

But in our hearts, we know our sin problem runs much deeper than a list of bad habits. All of us have rebelled against God. We have ignored him and have decided to run our own lives in a way that makes sense to us. The Bible says that the God who created us wants us to follow his plan for our lives. But because of our sin problem, we think our ideas and plans are better than his.

- *"For all have sinned and fall short of the glory of God"* (Romans 3:23).

What does it mean to "fall short of the glory of God"? It means that none of us has trusted and treasured God the way we should. We have sought to satisfy ourselves with other things and have treated those things as more valuable than God. We have gone our own way. According to the Bible, we have to pay a penalty for our sin. We cannot simply do things the way we choose and hope it will all be OK with God. Following our own plan leads to our destruction.

- *"There is a way that seems right to a man, but in the end it leads to death"* (Proverbs 14:12).

- *"For the wages of sin is death"* (Romans 6:23a).

The penalty for sin is that we are forever separated from God's love. God is holy, and we are sinful. No matter how hard we try, we cannot come up with some plan, like living a good life or even trying to do what the Bible says, and hope that we can avoid the penalty.

God's Solution to Sin

Thankfully God has a way to solve our dilemma. He became a man through the person of Jesus Christ. He lived a holy life, in perfect obedience to God's plan. He also willingly died on a cross to pay our penalty for sin. Then he proved that he is more powerful than sin or death by rising from the dead. He alone has the power to overrule the penalty for our sin.

- *"Jesus answered, 'I am the way and the truth and the life. No one comes to the Father except through me'"* (John 14:6).

- *"But God demonstrates his own love for us in this: While we were still sinners, Christ died for us"* (Romans 5:8).

- *"Christ died for our sins...he was buried...he was raised on the third day according to the Scriptures...he appeared to Peter, and then to the Twelve. After that, he appeared to more than five hundred"* (1 Corinthians 15:3-6).

- *"For the wages of sin is death, but the gift of God is eternal life in Christ Jesus our Lord"* (Romans 6:23).

The death of Jesus has fixed our sin problem. He has bridged the gap between God and us. He is calling all of us to come to him and to give up our own flawed plan for how to run our lives. He wants us to trust God and his plan.

Accepting God's Solution

If you agree that you are separated from God, he is calling you to confess your sins. All of us have made messes of our lives because we have stubbornly preferred our ideas and plans over his. As a result, we deserve to be cut off from God's love and his care for us. But God has promised that if we will agree that we have rebelled against his plan for us and have messed up our lives, he will forgive us and will fix our sin problem.

- *"Yet to all who received him, to those who believed in his name, he gave the right to become children of God"* (John 1:12).

- *"For it is by grace you have been saved, through*

faith—and this not from yourselves, it is the gift of
God—not by works, so that no one can boast"
(Ephesians 2:8-9).

When the Bible talks about receiving Christ, it means we acknowledge that we are sinners and that we can't fix the problem ourselves. It means we turn away from our sin. And it means we trust Christ to forgive our sins and to make us the kind of people he wants us to be. It's not enough to just intellectually believe that Christ is the Son of God. We must trust in him and his plan for our lives by faith, as an act of the will.

Are things right between you and God, with him and his plan at the center of your life? Or is life spinning out of control as you seek to make your way on your own?

You can decide today to make a change. You can turn to Christ and allow him to transform your life. All you need to do is to talk to him and tell him what is stirring in your mind and in your heart. If you've never done this, consider taking the steps listed here:

- Do you agree that you need God? Tell God.

- Have you made a mess of your life by following your own plan? Tell God.

- Do you want God to forgive you? Tell God.

- Do you believe that Jesus' death on the cross and his resurrection from the dead gave him the power to fix your sin problem and to grant you the free gift of eternal life? Tell God.

- Are you ready to acknowledge that God's plan for your life is better than any plan you could come up with? Tell God.

- Do you agree that God has the right to be the Lord and

master of your life? Tell God.

> *"Seek the Lord while he may be found;*
> *call on him while he is near"*
> (Isaiah 55:6).

Following is a suggested prayer:

> *Lord Jesus, I need you. Thank you for dying on the*
> *cross for my sins. I receive you as my Savior and Lord.*
> *Thank you for forgiving my sins and giving me eternal*
> *life. Make me the kind of person you want me to be.*

Does this prayer express the desire of your heart? If it does, pray it right now, and Christ will come into your life, as he promised.

Part Two: Living the Christian Life

For a person who is a follower of Christ—a Christian—the penalty for sin is paid in full. But the effect of sin continues throughout our lives.

- *"If we claim to be without sin, we deceive ourselves and the truth is not in us"* (1 John 1:8).

- *"For what I do is not the good I want to do; no, the evil I do not want to do—this I keep on doing"* (Romans 7:19).

The effects of sin carry over into our marriages as well. Even Christians struggle to maintain solid, God-honoring marriages. Most couples eventually realize that they can't do it on their own. But with God's help, they can succeed. The Holy Spirit can have a huge impact in the marriages of Christians who live constantly, moment by moment, under his gracious direction.

Self-Centered Christians

Many Christians struggle to live the Christian life in their own strength because they are not allowing God to control their lives. Their interests are self-directed, often resulting in failure and frustration.

- *"Brothers, I could not address you as spiritual but as worldly—mere infants in Christ. I gave you milk, not solid food, for you were not yet ready for it. Indeed, you are still not ready. You are still worldly. For since there is jealousy and quarreling among you, are you not worldly? Are you not acting like mere men?"* (1 Corinthians 3:1-3).

The self-centered Christian cannot experience the abundant and fruitful Christian life. Such people trust in their own efforts to live the Christian life: They are either uninformed about—or have forgotten—God's love, forgiveness, and power. This kind of Christian:

- has an up-and-down spiritual experience.

- cannot understand himself—he wants to do what is right, but cannot.

- fails to draw upon the power of the Holy Spirit to live the Christian life.

Some or all of the following traits may characterize the Christian who does not fully trust God:

Disobedience	Plagued by impure thoughts
Lack of love for God and others	Jealous
	Worrisome
Inconsistent prayer life	Easily discouraged, frustrated
Lack of desire for Bible study	Critical
Legalistic attitude	Lack of purpose

Note: The individual who professes to be a Christian but who continues to practice sin should realize that he may not be a Christian at all, according to 1 John 2:3; 3:6, 9; Ephesians 5:5.

Spirit-Centered Christians

When a Christian puts Christ on the throne of his life, he yields to God's control. This Christian's interests are directed by the Holy Spirit, resulting in harmony with God's plan.

- *"But the fruit of the Spirit is love, joy, peace, patience, kindness, goodness, faithfulness, gentleness and self-control. Against such things there is no law"* (Galatians 5:22-23).

Jesus said:

- *"I have come that they may have life, and have it to the full"* (John 10:10b).

- *"I am the vine; you are the branches. If a man remains in me and I in him, he will bear much fruit; apart from me you can do nothing"* (John 15:5).

- *"But you will receive power when the Holy Spirit comes on you; and you will be my witnesses in Jerusalem, and in all Judea and Samaria, and to the ends of the earth"* (Acts 1:8).

The following traits result naturally from the Holy Spirit's work in our lives:

Christ centered	Love
Holy Spirit empowered	Joy
Motivated to tell others about Jesus	Peace
	Patience
Dedicated to prayer	Kindness
Student of God's Word	Goodness
Trusts God	Faithfulness
Obeys God	Gentleness
	Self-control

The degree to which these traits appear in a Christian's life and marriage depends upon the extent to which the Christian trusts the Lord with every detail of life, and upon that person's maturity in Christ. One who is only beginning to understand the ministry of the Holy Spirit should not be discouraged if he is not as fruitful as mature Christians who have known and experienced this truth for a longer period of time.

Giving God Control

Jesus promises his followers an abundant and fruitful life as they allow themselves to be directed and empowered by the Holy Spirit. As we give God control of our lives, Christ lives in and through us in the power of the Holy Spirit (John 15).

If you sincerely desire to be directed and empowered by God, you can turn your life over to the control of the Holy Spirit right now (Matthew 5:6; John 7:37-39).

First, confess your sins to God, agreeing with him that you want to turn from any past sinful patterns in your life. Thank God in faith that he has forgiven all of your sins because Christ died for you (Colossians 2:13-15; 1 John 1:9; 2:1-3; Hebrews 10:1-18).

Be sure to offer every area of your life to God (Romans 12:1-2). Consider what areas you might rather keep to yourself, and be sure you're willing to give God control in those areas.

By faith, commit yourself to living according to the Holy Spirit's guidance and power.

- *Live by the Spirit: "So I say, live by the Spirit, and you will not gratify the desires of the sinful nature. For the sinful nature desires what is contrary to the Spirit, and the Spirit what is contrary to the sinful nature. They are in conflict with each other, so that you do not do what you want"* (Galatians 5:16-17).

- *Trust in God's Promise: "This is the confidence we have in approaching God: that if we ask anything according to his will, he hears us. And if we know that he hears us—whatever we ask—we know that we have what we asked of him"* (1 John 5:14-15).

Expressing Your Faith Through Prayer

Prayer is one way of expressing your faith to God. If the prayer that follows expresses your sincere desire, consider praying the prayer or putting the thoughts into your own words:

Dear God, I need you. I acknowledge that I have been directing my own life and that, as a result, I have sinned against you. I thank you that you have forgiven my sins through Christ's death on the cross for me. I now invite Christ to take his place on the throne of my life. Take control of my life through the Holy Spirit as you promised you would if I asked in faith. I now thank you for directing my life and for empowering me through the Holy Spirit.

Walking in the Spirit

If you become aware of an area of your life (an attitude or an action) that is displeasing to God, simply confess your sin, and thank God that he has forgiven your sins on the basis of Christ's death on the cross. Accept God's love and forgiveness by faith, and continue to have fellowship with him.

If you find that you've taken back control of your life through sin—a definite act of disobedience—try this exercise, "Spiritual Breathing," as you give that control back to God.

1. Exhale. Confess your sin. Agree with God that you've sinned against him, and thank him for his forgiveness of it, according to 1 John 1:9 and Hebrews 10:1-25. Remember that confession involves repentance, a determination to change attitudes and actions.

2. Inhale. Surrender control of your life to Christ, inviting the Holy Spirit to once again take charge. Trust that he now directs and empowers you, according to the command of Galatians 5:16-17 and the promise of 1 John 5:14-15. Returning to your faith in God enables you to continue to experience God's love and forgiveness.

Revolutionizing Your Marriage

This new commitment of your life to God will enrich your marriage. Sharing with your spouse what you've committed to is a powerful step in solidifying your own commitment. As you exhibit the Holy Spirit's work within you, your spouse may be drawn to make the same commitment you've made. If both of you have given control of your life to the Holy Spirit, you'll be able to help each other remain true to God, and your marriage may be revolutionized. With God in charge of your lives, life becomes an amazing adventure.

Leader's Notes

Contents

About Leading a HomeBuilders Group **112**

About the Sessions **116**

About the Leader's Notes..**118**

Session One **119**

Session Two...**122**

Session Three **125**

Session Four **129**

Session Five...**132**

Session Six **127**

Session Seven **140**

About Leading a HomeBuilders Group

What is the leader's job?

Your role is that of "facilitator"—one who encourages people to think and to discover what Scripture says, who helps group members feel comfortable, and who keeps things moving forward.

What is the best setting and time schedule for this study?

This study is designed as a small-group home Bible study. However, it can be adapted for use in a Sunday school setting as well. Here are some suggestions for using this study in a small group and in a Sunday school class:

In a small group

To create a friendly and comfortable atmosphere, it is recommended that you do this study in a home setting. In many cases the couple that leads the study also serves as host to the group. Sometimes involving another couple as host is a good idea. Choose the option you believe will work best for your group, taking into account factors such as the number of couples participating and the location.

Each session is designed as a ninety-minute study; but we recommend a two-hour block of time. This will allow you to move through each part of the study at a more relaxed pace. However, be sure to keep in mind one of the cardinal rules of a small group: Good groups start *and* end on time. People's time is valuable, and your group will appreciate you being respectful of this.

In a Sunday school class

There are two important adaptations you need to make if you want to use this study in a class setting: 1) The material you cover should focus on the content from the Blueprints section of each session. Blueprints is the heart of each session and is designed to last sixty minutes. 2) Most Sunday school classes are taught in a teacher format instead of a small group format. If this study will be used in a class setting, the class should adapt to a small group dynamic. This will involve an interactive, discussion-based format and may also require a class to break into multiple smaller groups (we recommend groups of six to eight people).

What is the best size group?

We recommend from four to eight couples (including you and your spouse). If you have more people interested than you think you can accommodate, consider asking someone else to lead a second group. If you have a large group, you are encouraged at various times in the study to break into smaller subgroups. This helps you cover the material in a timely fashion and allows for optimum interaction and participation within the group.

What about refreshments?

Many groups choose to serve refreshments, which help create an environment of fellowship. If you plan on including refreshments in your study, here are a couple of suggestions: 1) For the first session (or two) you should provide the refreshments and then allow the group to be involved by having people sign up to bring them on later dates. 2) Consider starting your group with a short time of informal fellowship and refreshments (fifteen minutes), then move into the study. If couples are late, they miss only the food and don't disrupt the study. You may also want to have refreshments available at the end of your meeting to encourage fellowship, but remember, respect the group members' time by ending the study on schedule and allowing anyone who needs to leave right away the opportunity to do so gracefully.

What about child care?

Groups handle this differently depending on their needs. Here are a couple of options you may want to consider:

- Have everyone be responsible for making their own arrangements.

- As a group, hire child care, and have all the kids watched in one location.

What about prayer?

An important part of a small group is prayer. However, as the leader, you need to be sensitive to the level of comfort the people in your group have toward praying in front of others. Never call on people to pray aloud if you don't know if they are comfortable doing this. There are a number of creative approaches you can take, such as modeling prayer, calling for volunteers, and letting people state their prayers in the form of finishing a sentence. A tool that is helpful in a group is a prayer list. You are encouraged to do this, but let it be someone else's ministry to the group. You should lead the prayer time, but allow another couple in the group the opportunity to create, update, and distribute prayer lists.

In closing

An excellent resource that covers leading a HomeBuilders group in greater detail is the *HomeBuilders Leader Guide* by Drew and Kit Coons. This book may be obtained at your local Christian bookstore, or by contacting Group Publishing or FamilyLife.

About the Sessions

Each session in this study is composed of the following categories: Warm-Up, Blueprints, Wrap-Up, and HomeBuilders Project. A description of each of these categories is as follows:

Warm-Up (15 minutes)

The purpose of Warm-Up is to help people unwind from a busy day and get to know each other better. Typically the first activity in Warm-Up is an exercise that is meant to be fun while introducing the topic of the session. The ability to share in fun with others is important in building relationships. Another component of Warm-Up is the second part (except in Session One), which is designed to provide accountability for the HomeBuilders Project that is to be completed by couples between sessions.

Blueprints (60 minutes)

This is the heart of the study. In this part of each session, people answer questions related to the topic of study and look to God's Word for understanding. Some of the questions are to be answered by couples, in subgroups, or in the group at large. There are notes in the margin or instructions within a question that designate these groupings.

Wrap-Up (15 minutes)

This category serves to "bring home the point" and wind down a session in an appropriate fashion.

HomeBuilders Project (60 minutes)

This project is the unique application step in a HomeBuilders study. Before leaving a meeting, couples are encouraged to "Make a Date" to do this project prior to the next meeting. Each HomeBuilders Project contains three sections: 1) As a Couple—a brief exercise designed to start the date in a fun way; 2) Individually—a section of questions for husbands and wives to answer separately; 3) Interact as a Couple—an opportunity for couples to share their answers with each other and to make application in their lives.

In addition to the above regular features, occasional activities are labeled "For Extra Impact." These activities provide a more active or visual way to make a particular point. Be mindful that people in a group have different learning styles. While most of what is presented in these sessions is verbal, a visual or active exercise now and then helps engage more of the senses and appeals to people who learn best by seeing, touching, and doing.

About the Leader's Notes

The sessions in this study can be easily led without a lot of preparation time. However, accompanying Leader's Notes have been provided to assist you in preparation. The categories within the Leader's Notes are as follows:

Objectives

The purpose of the Objectives is to help focus the issues that will be presented in each session.

Notes and Tips

This section will relate any general comments about the session. This information should be viewed as ideas, helps, and suggestions. You may want to create a checklist of things you want to be sure to do in each session.

Commentary

Included in this section are notes that relate specifically to Blueprints questions. Not all Blueprints questions in each session will have accompanying commentary notes. Questions with related commentaries are designated by numbers. (For example, Blueprints question 3 in Session One corresponds to number 3 in the Commentary section of Session One Leader's Notes.)

Session One:
Overcoming Isolation

Objectives

Defeating selfishness and isolation is essential in building oneness and a God-honoring marriage.

In this session, couples will...

- share enjoyable experiences from marriage.

- identify selfishness as the cause of isolation in marriage.

- affirm their awareness that God has a plan for overcoming isolation and selfishness in marriage.

- choose a specific step to take to work on defeating selfishness.

Notes and Tips

1. If you have not already done so, you will want to read "About Leading a HomeBuilders Group," "About the Sessions," and "About the Leader's Notes" starting on page 112.

2. As part of the first session you may want to review with the group some Ground Rules (see page 11 in the Introduction).

3. This first session contains a For Extra Impact exercise that you can use as an additional Warm-Up activity if you desire. If you use this activity, be sure to watch your time so the session stays on track.

4. Because this is the first session, make a special point to tell the group about the importance of the HomeBuilders Project. Encourage each couple to "Make a Date" for a time before the next meeting to complete the project. Mention that you will ask about this during Warm-Up of the next session.

5. This is the first session, so you may want to offer a closing prayer instead of asking others to pray aloud. Many people are uncomfortable praying in front of others, and unless you already know your group well, it may be wise to slowly venture into various methods of prayer. Regardless of how you decide to close, you should serve as a model.

6. You may want to remind the group that because this group is just under way, it is not too late to invite another couple to join the group. Challenge everyone to think about couples they could invite to the next session.

Commentary

Here is some additional information about various Blueprints questions. Note: The numbers below correspond to the Blueprints questions of the same numbers in the session. If you share any of these points, be sure to do so in a manner that does not stifle discussion by making you the authority with the real answers. Begin your comments by saying things like, "One thing I notice in this passage is..." or, "I think another reason for this is..."

3. Isaiah 53:6: "turned to his own way," which is selfishness.

5. Isolation can result in misunderstanding, pride, frustration, sexual and emotional dissatisfaction, and many other symptoms of a troubled marriage. If your group members have trouble coming up with effects of isolation, you may want to share these possible answers.

6. To some people, overcoming isolation seems too difficult a task. Also, they may fear rejection from their spouses.

9. Mark 10:35-45 says it is necessary to serve in order to build anything great. This account is also told in Matthew 20:20-28.

Session Two:
Creating Oneness

Objectives

Oneness in marriage is achieved as both husband and wife obey God and work together in building their home from the same set of blueprints: the Bible.

In this session, couples will...

- discover the benefits of oneness in marriage.

- identify commitment to God's blueprints as the key to achieving oneness and harmony in marriage.

- evaluate how God's blueprints for marriage are being followed in their homes.

- plan specific ways in which to mirror God's image better in their marriages.

Notes and Tips

1. Session One focused on problems in a marriage. This session begins exploring God's blueprints for the solution to selfishness and isolation. Be sensitive to individuals or couples who struggle with accepting God's purposes as their own. Your warmth and acceptance can play a significant role in someone's decision to truly consider the principles of these sessions.

2. You may wish to have extra study guides and Bibles available for those who came to the session without them.

3. If someone joins the group for the first time in this session, give a brief summary of the main points of Session One. Also be sure to introduce people who do not know each other. You may want to have each new couple answer Warm-Up question 1 from Session One.

4. If refreshments are planned for this session, make sure arrangements for them are covered.

5. If your group has decided to utilize a prayer list, make sure this is covered.

6. If you told the group during the first session that you'd be asking them to share something they learned from the first HomeBuilders Project, be sure to follow through by asking if anyone would like to share something about the project.

7. You will notice that a margin note with the Blueprint questions suggests breaking into smaller groups if there is a large number of people in your group. Smaller groups will help facilitate discussion and participation.

8. You may want to ask for a volunteer or two to close the session in prayer. Check ahead of time with a couple of people you think might be comfortable praying aloud.

Commentary

Note: The numbers that follow correspond to the Blueprints questions of the same numbers in the session.

4. If your group needs help getting the discussion going, here are some possible answers you may want to share: by working hard at it; by improving your sex life; by each person taking his or her share of household responsibilities; and by working on the relationship.

5. Involving God in a relationship. Obedience to God's Word.

6. Paul's instructions call for putting others' interests above those of ourselves. This is critical for achieving unity, or oneness, in marriage.

8. Genesis 1:27: God made two distinctly different humans (male and female) so that together they would reflect the image of God.

Genesis 1:28: God created men and women as his ambassadors to glorify him on earth and to tell others (friends, co-workers, neighbors) about the need to follow Christ.

Genesis 2:18: Companionship replaces isolation.

Session Three:
Receiving Your Spouse

Objectives

Oneness in marriage requires receiving your spouse as God's perfect provision for your needs.

In this session, couples will...

- identify the ways Adam needed Eve and compare those with ways they need their mates.

- discuss the importance and the basis of receiving their mates as God's perfect provision.

- analyze how weaknesses in mates have an impact on receiving them as God's provision.

- affirm specific ways they and their mates need each other and can accept one another as God's gift.

Notes and Tips

1. By the third session your group members should know one another well enough to feel somewhat relaxed and comfortable in talking with each other—at least about external aspects of their marriages. This session probes some very sensitive areas, exploring ways that we need our mates. Some people may have difficulty admitting these ways to themselves or to their mates, let alone to other people. Your role here, providing acceptance and support without pressing anyone, is crucial. Pray for sensitivity to each person as a unique being. And remind people that they can pass on any question they prefer not to answer.

2. A For Extra Impact activity in the Wrap-Up calls for various household tools. If you plan to do this exercise, you will need to gather before the meeting an assortment of tools with two parts, such as pliers, scissors, hedge clippers, a manual can opener, and the like. Gather at least one tool per couple.

3. The HomeBuilders Project for this session involves writing a love letter. If there are couples in your group who have attended a FamilyLife Marriage Conference, they may have previously done this exercise. If this is the case and it is brought up, ask the question: Can a person ever write too many love letters to his or her beloved?

4. Remember the importance of starting and ending on time.

5. You may find it helpful to make some notes right after the meeting to help you evaluate how things went. Ask yourself questions such as: Did everyone participate? Is there anyone that I should make a special effort to follow up with before the next session? Asking yourself questions like these will help you focus.

6. As a model to the group, it is important that you complete the HomeBuilders Project before each session.

Commentary

2. To keep him from feeling self-sufficient. To enable him to recognize his need for God and for his mate.

Note: The numbers that follow correspond to the Blueprints questions of the same numbers in the session.

3. What follows is how some commentators develop the meaning of Genesis 2:21-22. You may want to share these thoughts with your group.

Caused Adam to sleep: Some people speculate that the sleep made the surgical procedure easier and kept Adam from offering unwanted advice about the woman's design.

Took a rib: This implies God recognized the equality of woman with man and depicts the strong emotional bonds between the sexes.

Closed the flesh: Adam was not harmed by this endeavor.

Made a woman: She was totally God's handiwork.

Brought her to Adam: God was obviously concerned about Adam's response to the woman and wanted her to be recognized as coming from God.

6. Obviously Eve was the only woman there, and we also can assume there was an immediate attraction between them. However, the only clue given in the passage is that Adam must have recognized that God was presenting her as a gift from God. Adam trusted in the God who had created him and who had now provided a mate for him.

8. If the issue of spouse abuse is raised, call attention to these Scriptures that provide wise counsel: Romans 13:1

and 1 Peter 2:13-15 teach God's establishment of governmental authority to control those who do wrong. A person in danger should not hesitate to contact the authorities for protection. Romans 5:8 shares Christ's example of loving the sinner even though hating sin (Psalm 45:7). One spouse's wrong acts do not excuse retaliation by the other. Proverbs 14:7 says to "stay away from a foolish man." This does not mean divorce; it simply advises establishing enough space to avoid the influence of the fool.

9. Note: Rejection of the gift is rejection of the giver.

It's possible someone may ask, "When we were married, neither of us even knew God, let alone trusted him. How could my spouse be God's gift to me under that circumstance?" Refer the question to the group to answer. As you discuss this question, mention that the Scriptures clearly show that God is sovereign in the affairs of individuals and nations.

10. You can regard your spouse's weaknesses as opportunities for you to be needed and as tools of God to cause you to trust him. Also, you should realize that some weaknesses will probably never be changed, and those that are changed will only occur in a climate of loving acceptance.

Session Four:
Constructing a
Relationship

Objectives

Building your marriage involves a process of leaving parents, uniting with each other, and becoming one.

In this session, couples will...

- define the importance of leaving parents.

- discuss ways in which spouses unite with each other.

- identify the connection between becoming one and achieving oneness.

Notes and Tips

1. Congratulations. With the completion of this session, you will be more than halfway through this study. It's time for a checkup: How are you feeling? How is the group going? What has worked well so far? What things might you consider changing as you head into the second half?

2. One of the topics discussed in this session is leaving parents. On an issue like this, it is easy for the focus to shift to a discussion about in-laws. While this may be interesting, it is not the point and should be avoided. If this happens, gently direct the discussion back toward the topic at hand by encouraging couples to think in terms of the relationship with one's own parents.

Also, you may want to emphasize to the group that no longer being dependent on parents does not necessarily mean not receiving help or assistance at times. For example, a couple could borrow money from parents. This transaction would probably not indicate dependence on parents if it is handled in a businesslike manner with an agreed-upon plan for repayment which is then honored. Nor would parental help in a crisis necessarily indicate undue dependence. But a pattern of going to parents for repeated assistance is a serious danger signal.

3. You and your spouse may want to write notes of thanks and encouragement to the couples in your group this week. Thank them for their commitment and contribution, and let them know you are praying for them. (Make a point to pray for them as you write their note.)

4. By this time, group members should be getting more comfortable with each other. For prayer at the end of this session, you may want to give anyone an opportunity to pray by asking the group to finish a sentence that goes something like this: "Lord, I want to thank you for _____." Be sensitive to anyone who may not feel comfortable doing this.

5. Looking ahead: For Blueprints in Session Five, men and women will be in two different groups. For this part of the study, you will need to have a person lead the group you're not in. Be sure to line this up prior to that session. Your spouse may be a good choice for this.

Commentary

3. When your parents are too clingy, you may not mature. Your spouse may develop resentments that create conflicts.

Note: The numbers that follow correspond to the Blueprints questions of the same numbers in the session.

When you are dependent on parents and not on your husband or wife, your spouse is not allowed to meet your needs, thus thwarting oneness in your relationship.

4. Pray for your parents. Write and call them regularly. Organize special events to honor them. Put together a special, written tribute to your parents. Care for them when your help is needed.

If any couples in your group have parents who are elderly and becoming incapable of caring for themselves, you may want to ask, "How can a couple balance responsibilities to each other with the needs of aging parents?" (Although one's spouse must always be given first priority, that should not be made into an excuse to neglect responsibility to parents. See Mark 7:6-13 for Jesus' accusation against those who used their religious vows as an excuse to avoid caring for their parents.)

5. Being united to your spouse means making a special, lifelong commitment to that person. A couple cannot make this type of commitment if they have not truly left their parents.

8. Physical union is an expression of oneness with the total person, uniting spirit, soul, and body.

10. This meant more than their physical nakedness. It also meant they were completely "transparent" with one another, feeling no threat in revealing themselves to one another.

Session Five:
Fitting Together

Objectives

God wants husbands and wives to assume biblical responsibilities within their marriages.

In this session, couples will...

- identify the biblical responsibilities husbands and wives have to one another.

- discuss things that interfere with fulfilling these responsibilities.

- develop a job description to provide guidance in fulfilling these responsibilities.

Notes and Tips

1. For this session the men and women will be in separate groups for Blueprints. Make sure you have asked someone to help facilitate the discussion for the group that you are not in. You will also want to encourage the person helping you to review the Commentary notes related to the Blueprints questions that person will be responsible for leading.

2. In this session you will tackle one of the most difficult and controversial topics today in the Church—roles of husbands and wives. Most couples do not clearly understand what the Bible says about roles and will come in with preconceived ideas. More than anything else, you'll want to challenge them to set aside their preconceived ideas and look at what the Bible says about these subjects—not at what they think or what the culture thinks.

3. Because of the subject being discussed, it is quite possible for a group to spend a lot of time on one question. However, it is important for you as group leader to politely keep things moving forward. In particular, be sure to allow time for the last question in Blueprints to be answered. This is key because it becomes the point of discussion between husbands and wives in the Wrap-Up.

4. As the leader of a small group, one of the best things you can do for your group is to pray specifically for each member. Why not take some time to do this as you prepare for this session?

Commentary

Blueprints for Husbands

Note: In preparing for this session, be sure you have reviewed points 2 and 3 in the preceding Notes and Tips.

Note: The numbers that follow correspond to the Blueprints questions of the same numbers in the session.

If some men begin to vent frustrations about their wives or about women in general, explain that the focus of this session is not on pointing out where our wives may be off base, but on discovering ways men can become more successful as husbands.

1. Husband, father, provider, lover, sensitive and caring, employer or employee, and so forth. Success today is usually evaluated not in terms of our relationships, but of our status at work, the size of our house, and the accumulation of wealth.

2. You may want to bring out the point that many men's fathers did not provide effective role models as husbands and, after years of attacks on the roles of men and women in our culture, many men are unsure about how to relate to their wives.

5. The husband loves and cares for the wife as Christ loves and cares for the church. Unselfish love is always demonstrated by giving of self, not just of things. Many wives have not seen their husbands deny themselves since courtship, and many others have never seen it at all. A husband's unselfish love frees the wife from her own selfishness, defeating isolation and building oneness.

7. Mark 10:42-45: Jesus made a clear contrast between the superior leader, who focuses on authority and status, and the servant-leader, who focuses on giving of self to the ones he leads. The servant-leader does not lord authority over others but willingly serves the needs of all. He does not demand service from others; rather, he gives up his own life and desires for others to have life—whether they deserve it or not.

8. If a man tends to be passive, it would mean taking his responsibilities seriously and beginning to initiate opportunities to serve his wife and meet her needs.

A dictatorial husband would need to begin looking for ways to serve instead of to dominate. He would involve his wife in decisions and would be concerned with her fulfillment.

Blueprints for Wives

Note: In preparing for this session, be sure you have reviewed points 2 and 3 in the preceding Notes and Tips.

Note: The numbers that follow correspond to the Blueprints questions of the same numbers in the session.

Be aware that as women gather, each one has different needs. If a woman expresses anger or bitterness, thank her for being open with the group, then ask her to hold off making any final judgments until she has had an opportunity to consider the complete teaching of this session.

Some women may want to vent frustrations about their husbands. Explain that the focus of this session will not be on pointing out where husbands are off base, but on discovering specific ways to become successful as a wife.

4. This passage causes a negative reaction in many women today. It conjures up images of a husband ordering his wife around and forcing her to do his will, and the wife meekly responding to his every wish. Most arguments against roles in marriage stem from the fact that many husbands throughout history have been dictatorial leaders. However, that's not what the Bible teaches.

6. The word "submission" comes from Greek words that mean "under" and "arrange." The sense of the term is to voluntarily organize or fit under.

Submission does not require a wife to violate other scriptural commands or principles. The Bible does not ask wives to submit to sinful or damaging demands. If the issue of spousal abuse is raised, suggest these passages that provide wise counsel:

Proverbs 14:7 says to "stay away from a foolish man." This does not mean divorce; it simply advises making enough space to avoid the influence of the fool.

Romans 13:1 and 1 Peter 2:13-15 teach God's establishment of governmental authority to control those who do wrong. A wife in danger should not hesitate to contact the authorities for protection.

Session Six:
Building in the Spirit

Objectives

A husband and wife can experience true oneness only as they live by faith, in the power of the Holy Spirit.

In this session, couples will...

- contrast a marriage without God and a marriage with God.

- identify key elements necessary for walking with the Holy Spirit.

- discuss ways to restore and maintain a relationship with the Holy Spirit.

- pray, with everyone asking for God's power in their lives.

Notes and Tips

1. Realizing it is impossible to fully cover all the truth regarding the Holy Spirit in one session, the points covered here are intended to encourage individuals and couples to begin to experience the power of the Holy Spirit as an essential step in a lifelong process of Christian growth. For further study on this essential topic of Christian living, some excellent small group studies are available from Campus Crusade for Christ.

2. Consider arranging for a group member—or your spouse—to share briefly about the Holy Spirit's ministry in his or her life and marriage. Meet with this person ahead of time to review what will be shared, making sure it will be brief, practical, and supportive of the concepts in this session.

3. If you sense that someone in your group is not a Christian, this might be a good time to take a few moments to explain briefly how you became a Christian and the difference that walking with Christ has made in your life. You can also refer group members to the article "Our Problems, God's Answers" in their books.

4. This session contains two For Extra Impact exercises. The first is a Warm-Up activity that you may want to do. The second is included at the end of this session (after the HomeBuilders Project). It would be appropriate to suggest to group members that they consider doing the second exercise at some point, perhaps as part of their personal quiet time.

5. For Wrap-Up, you will lead the group in a time of prayer. You may want to pray the prayer in Wrap-Up aloud, or you may just want to allow time for silent prayer. After allowing for this time of prayer, you may want to spend the rest of the Wrap-Up time in further prayer as a whole group, or with spouses praying together. Another option would be to ask the question, "Does anyone have something they would like to share?"

6. Looking ahead: For the next session—the last session of this study—you may want to have someone, or a couple, from the group plan on sharing what this study or the group has meant to them. If this is something you would like to do, be thinking about whom you might ask in advance to share.

Commentary

1. After hearing people's answer to this question, you might want to ask the follow-up question: "What do you see as the source of our problems in carrying out our good intentions in our lives and marriages?"

> **Note:** The numbers that follow correspond to the Blueprints questions of the same numbers in the session.

3. Many people interpret this passage as reflecting three kinds of people, of which everyone falls into one of these three categories:

- The natural person (1 Corinthians 2:14)—one who does not have a personal relationship with Christ.

- The Spirit-centered Christian (1 Corinthians 2:15-16)— one who knows Christ and submits to God's direction.

- The self-centered Christian (1 Corinthians 3:1-3)—one who knows Christ yet has not matured as a Christian and lives a self-directed life.

6. The purposes for which God designed marriage cannot be achieved apart from his presence. The Holy Spirit is God's personal presence in your marriage. Intimacy with the Holy Spirit will release God's power in an individual and a marriage and will enable a couple to overcome the barriers to his purpose of oneness.

Session Seven:
Building a Legacy

Objectives

Building a God-honoring legacy requires that you determine together to influence your world and future generations for Christ.

In this session, couples will...

- compare a worldly legacy with a God-honoring legacy.

- identify the spiritual and physical legacies a marriage can leave.

- evaluate the direction of life and marriage and choose desired legacies to build.

- discuss specific actions that can be taken to build a God-honoring legacy.

Notes and Tips

1. It is crucial that you approach this seventh session as an opportunity to encourage couples to take specific steps beyond this series to keep their marriages growing. For example, you may want to challenge couples who have developed the habit of a "date night" during the course of this study to continue this practice.

While this HomeBuilders Couples Series has great value in itself, people are likely to gradually return to their previous patterns of living unless they commit to a plan for carrying on the progress made. Continuing effort is required for people to initiate and maintain new directions in their marriage. One choice this group may be interested in is doing another study from this series.

2. If your group includes childless couples, focus most of your attention during this session on spiritual descendants rather than physical descendants. Also, if there are couples whose children are grown or nearly grown and who are not serving Christ, encourage those parents that God is still able to overrule any mistakes made in earlier years. Encourage these parents to confess their errors to God—and to their children. This can be a powerful means of restoring relationships and communication.

3. As a part of this session, you may want to consider devoting some time to plan for one more meeting—a party to celebrate the completion of this study!

Commentary

4. Joshua 24:14-15: family commitment to fear and serve God.

Psalm 112:1-2: fear the Lord and delight in his commands.

2 Timothy 1:5: sincere faith.

Note: The numbers that follow correspond to the Blueprints questions of the same numbers in the session.

3 John 4: walking in the truth.

5. 2 Timothy 2:2 stresses the importance of finding faithful men to build your life into, with the goal of helping them do the same with other faithful men. Matthew 28:19-20 instructs us to reach out to those in our world to make disciples.

6. A God-honoring legacy is obviously more than just physical reproduction. God's purpose is not just more people, but people committed to God. Deuteronomy 6 shows that this is accomplished as parents tell and show God's truth to their children in the midst of everyday living.

7. If people struggle to answer this question, you may want to share the following suggested motivations:

Romans 8:31-39: No difficulty can separate us from Christ's love and protection; thus, we are assured that we will succeed when we depend on him.

1 Peter 3:9-16: God called us to be blessed; therefore, we are to pursue good, even when facing trouble.

2 Peter 3:8-15: God will end this present world; his patience is our opportunity.

8. A worldly heritage—even the best of this material world will be destroyed. A God-honoring heritage—God will reward those who build according to his blueprints.

$\mathcal{S}$ ince attending a FamilyLife Marriage Conference, the Martins' love really shows...

But who's keeping score?

FAMILYLIFE MARRIAGE CONFERENCE
Get away for a "Weekend to Remember"!

Chalk one up for your marriage! Get away to a FamilyLife Marriage Conference for a fun, meaningful weekend together. Learn how to understand your mate, build your marriage, and much more.

To register or receive more information,
visit www.familylife.com or call 1-800-FL-TODAY.

FAMILYLIFE™
Bringing Timeless Principles Home

Make Your Marriage the Best It Can Be!

Great marriages don't just happen—husbands and wives need to nurture them. They need to make their marriage relationship a priority.

That's where the **newly revised** HomeBuilders Couples Series® can help! The series consists of interactive 6- to 7-week small group studies that make it *easy* for couples to really open up with each other. The result is fun, non-threatening interactions that build stronger Christ-centered relationships between spouses—*and* with other couples!

Whether you've been married for years, or are newly married, this series will help you and your spouse discover timeless principles from God's Word that you can apply to your marriage and make it the best it can be!

ISBN 0-7644-2249-9

The HomeBuilders Leader Guide gives you all the information and encouragement you need to start and lead a dynamic HomeBuilders small group.

The HomeBuilders Couples Series® includes these life-changing studies:
HomeBuilders Leader Guide
Building Teamwork in Your Marriage
Building Your Marriage
Building Your Mate's Self-Esteem
Growing Together in Christ
Improving Communication in Your Marriage
Making Your Remarriage Last
Mastering Money in Your Marriage
Overcoming Stress in Your Marriage
Raising Children of Faith
Resolving Conflict in Your Marriage

FAMILYLIFE™
Bringing Timeless Principles Home
www.familylife.com

Look for the **HomeBuilders Couples Series®** at your local Christian bookstore or write:

P.O. Box 485, Loveland, CO 80539
www.grouppublishing.com